SCREEDS

SCREEDS

OF

STEPHEN WIEST

Odd Volumes

OF THE
Fortnightly Review

LES BROUZILS
2013

Odd Volumes of
The Fortnightly Review

Le Ligny
2 rue Georges Clemenceau
85260 Les Brouzils
France

ODD VOLUME 1
2013

ISBN 978-0615851587

SCREED:

A fragment cut torn or broken
from a main piece

A long roll or list

A lengthy discourse

A gossiping piece of writing

A piece of a literary work

A sound as of tearing

A drinking bout

A border of a woman's cap

IMPOSSIBLE RECONCILIATIONS
OCCUR OR NOT

on the weaving pathway of consciousness where patterns emerge through the chattering clouds of rumor, the news, and the slaughter to unfold a mind accruing beyond myth's opaque stare; recording images and obsessions, jostling and scraping, often unattended, sometimes for years, yet always cobbled with hope of discovery. The same concerns lift again and again, redirected here, there by loves and consequences. Age comes bringing lucidity of the right word, but also encouraging the forgetful boast. Age comes unwinding our past inventions, and bearing rumors of where our future lies. The story is old, these over-written images a humbling palimpsest of time, of language, laddering to a separate conscious–ness. It cannot be known in a day; it is only language playing, a consciousness made of words, amazing, terrorizing, stunning witless. Sometimes, setting down a copious joy, sometimes not. And so it must continue.

To those who find similar ambiguities...

PROLOGUE

Lately, there has grown a November mood,
a dark feather's touch, hinting
a coming weather when the night lengthens,
both dusk and dawn, making icy footsteps
on our sunny pathways moot.
So,
the miming bravado of our better selves
suffering any delay in grasping our wrongs
or admitting the heaped-up rubble of our desires,
pitting additions against vows,
is to stall
that certain day each will stand up, giddy
in the morning light and say, I'm old.

That touch (was it from a wing
high and southward seeking?)
brushing the cheek with a shock,
morphing beyond the usual lament,
foreshadows a cold time ahead—
those chill dawn thoughts of aging and ending
as though love's gone cold, gone friendly.

That's when,
that unmapped particle of galaxies within
brings the singing sense; singularity appears
from a center bearing words
back from my hot-blooded years,
that sense,
muse, memory, always thought as other—
a bloody sweeping opposite,
the lifeline of a poem;
I am not the only one cried out to you
searching the first note of all these songs.
We have, each one, been waiting for this ripening:
Each, Each... Each one.
Now shadows lighten, voices
rounding corners of the littered past urge me:

It's time to finish up.
Now you will see what I meant to have from you
Rather than memories of your green age,
Spoken through you from behind each mask,
As each mask tells you it is time to see and say.

ii

When the folded cloak of time
arcs a sudden summer rainbow,
when forgetting and impossible memories
reconcile and unfold
the exquisite panoply of our expanding
forever into the places we take light
where there is to be light,
shall I humbled say, "If…?"
or shall I say, "Only…?"

The stillness inside is the promise to meet
the hum of the body building these chords:
a throat tightening becomes words, becomes music—
sings:

You will become a thought flowing

With the thoughts that have no voice, no sayer.

Bear with me friend,
Let's tell the wonder of it, seeing
on imagined wings above the shifting wind
Clearly as various weathers will allow.

SCREEDS

I.

This roiling cloud, this consciousness...

I say you this poem   but quietly
after the silent confessions, and long
confrontations with an I, unstable as a top,
have spun out, from green baby steps,
through the puffed importance of harassing times
and the jelled humors from changeling peers;

now, I bend my legs cold mornings
before I try to walk again, and I embrace
this horde of doubts, all icy here and pitiless,
in the shambles of my white city,
        where dust seines the wind.

I wish and ask, without evocation, or appeal,

this desire; *Sans* a mutable sign turning
this bright zodiac, miming obsession's coiling serpent;
it is a simple question:
                    Will you listen, just listen?

Is there no saving sweetness, no limp of empathy
for greedy neighbors and dissolute friends?

Am I too abstract?
                    They told me so, do still.

Then, I knew so much—as when I said
I would die tomorrow like the great ones,
escaping the withered muscles,
the flaccid limbs under dry skin,
the heart beat arrhythmic as an old blues tune.

But here I am, covered by a thin coat
against this cold wind blowing, grateful.

Am I afraid of passion?
                    They told me so, still do;
Always, feelings translucent on demand.

Instead, I trust the quick tongue
To mark the dimple in her shoulder.

But said, "Yes,
>how I fear it,
>burning
through these decades
until only a guess
might take one beyond meaning—
>to sense there
>no escape."
"No escape?   False choice."
"No, No. I am not running,
>>I am not hiding."

I am a point with many directions,
and take them all outside of time;
what I say is gone, what I chisel
on the record of substance is time spent.

In the long lifeline, winding down milliseconds
in the rowdy market-stalls of language;
what can be said—words a consciousness
with limits, outside this consciousness
we never grasp.

Forget escape, but keep on running,
encountering others in the juice of choice,
and find each owns a topical wisdom
on a quivering balance, trying
to maintain our halting mottled skins,
and through persistent searching
perceive lightning in dark silent peripheries.

II.

Is no one else to speak for us,
No silky plot unravel
On this barrier island where
Unfolding vast horizons of our pride
To angels and demons,
Each night, we oblivious
Stalk the dead mimic's tune?

This funny wresting of individual thoughts,
This inflorescence
(the most elegant Distinction)

retorts

Another I,
It may be I, dissolved
In the luminous mist of the now,
Will stand and chant to rolling clouds

Now Now Now!

Until "At last," glows from brown winter
In the sunset dappled woods behind the house.

We reach out to touch the gnarled roots
In the deep clay of the headlands,
Where the ancient chill warns fingers,
Where roots' white tongues lick
The trace sustenance
To flash sap
to yawning buds lifting up
on empty limbs this hesitant April.

III.

If the Ace of Diamonds is cast, a fortuneteller's mark
into the fragrance of bay leaves, if there are spells
beside the hormones' exuberant romping,
perhaps, the consolation of our bodies
will be enough to release our unkempt wills,
even lying among leaves of the old year drifting,
forming a sense of the new year's shape.
Find us there among men, headstrong still,
after sidelong glances, among the women talking,
their stories of living, associations of change,
sickle and bounty.

The ample beauty of it all says
there continues a simple absence
as our connection and our awareness
make us ask, what is happening
to our connection and our place?

For absence is our constant sibling
carrying all future losses in the now,
to sweet daybreak through night-sweats shame,
in a compensation, in an expiation:

all that is prophecy and punished probably
by glibness and deceit in concepts falling
                into history,
the grotesque dancing before triumphal arches,
                into art, into slaughter and laughter.

When clowns guess each others' names
in the early evening show,
while the children wait the promised magic,
vain laughter and long processions will meld
in a compensation
        we shape trembling lips to name,
in an expiation which asks
        is this the absence
        we were preparing for?

So, let the sibilance and rhythms weigh
more than words, more
than an intermittent shaping
by a candle in the draft—
Where one leads, the others follow
crossing brown windy highlands
to drift down and drink from a pool
where one drowns in one's own reflection
or scatters one's reflection with a stone.

Where is your song then;
the one to host you through all weathers
when waters move, and your reflection, too?

IV.

To see love unwinding in wavering dreams,
who and what they were, how long how much
how they loved at all—these wild passions
across rollicking empires, slashing violence,
and our wild passion, like a taste of precious fruit.

I can feel it all again in wakefulness at dawn,
the indecision in this trickster, this guide of dreams,
amenable seduction

Historia

Artful, wide-legged and sublime.

Garlands of fruit on the laurel stake,
Embraced by the arc the finches make.

Thus, the precise finches of Darwin's tale
accommodate strange weather in strange lands.

When spring is only this moment green
and frost still webs the dawn's defining edges,
layered scenes, depicting ancient forms,
the makers there, man and woman,
become new again, the dream repeats.
So, in a continuous sameness of nights,
comfort lives in knowing where the terror lies.

V.

Come on, taste this vast world;
praise that privilege, and the chance
which must not be lost to harridans and louts;
small time each has will prove
we become our thoughts remembered,
as though others might dream them, too.

Desire; this beauty is the worth of each,
the riches we accrue in an infinite world.
We live, multiply, die
to pass our several parts around, clouds
suspended above this sparkle in dark imagining.

To each, the light bursting new buds
comes from the lost beginnings, unique,
incomprehensible in each antique spring,
this quantum of unknown acts
this random array of choice.

Amid transformations endless as flowers
moving in the south wind,
always in the act of return, endless as girls
whispering new worlds, endless as boys
storming the porch with plastic rifles,
dying into cowboys and crusaders, variorum heroes
in this playful common world,
which we should never leave,
where all the story's combinations may be lived,
where death is an early entrance to another story;
all possibilities occur across a cloudless afternoon,
occur as well, under the awning
on the porch in the rain.

VI.

Praise the old ones conjured from ancient cities.
Their reasons were loud and luxurious
as their lusts. Now, we bow as inheritors,
fractions of old stories rising,
their ruptured spaces gone misty
remembering each shout-out for glory.

From the foam of days
we spiral slowly down to a day like today;
taking hard measures, but arriving—
Ritual   controlled,
yet chance each time is still our better hope—
chance, still arises, a dark green slime,
from the north side of brooding forests,
staining the hands; still on our heels,
these tinkering chromosomes playing their game.

Now hear songs of the fey barbarians,
truckers and their fat and salty mates
watch rising waters fill their evenings
as their dreams float into that fog
where their children will not dream.
The formula changes from looking at yesterday,
looking for morning, to looking
where no memories arise.
They bring no lists of glory, nor can they
cause that smile, that mellow gentle sigh.
Shadows of stone knives descend
amid a few worked stones in the empty meadow.

VII.

I would fall into sleep if I could,
leaving these pieces of dream
in the sharp rubble of the cloning days.
Yet… but… so… whatever—
It is early here
tentative days warm slowly now

beside the woman
who has cried me a name
as I have given her a name—

My muse may be named
any of the names I have spoken smiling,
(it's attitude which will be blamed)
sometimes those names clipped by a sneer.
That ancient muse was moody, too;
as is mine, a lover flaunting or jealous,

it's all the same between us,
we're *au courant* in the seasons,
she is who she is; I invent some more of her
to sing songs, sadder the sooner smiled upon.

Be with me now
each to each   we vow
these words gathering, as seeds still silent
leading a sheltered life beneath the crusting soil.

O that there might be dancing for all of us
on dim islands on a far horizon.

VIII.

i.

I say you this confusion for itself, let it,
as changeling breezes, be the way we are.
Then, quietly bend to the turning glory—
Ritual, industry, *no stop, no '.', no nth value*,
no white robed priests, oil or blood.

Memories make us other people, sometimes
making us more than our bony frames can hold
laying down a memory today, or giving over, too,
on the same memory of you and a different day.
Still, we walk this land like the earliest ones,
our footprints in the marsh fill with water.
We build tomorrow pinching
The brighter parts of yesterday.

I roam many worlds
in this persistent dream, conscious of falling
but before that conscious of what I saw
tumbling with the two-faced mask
spinning round me, feckless dancer.

We are Hermes/Aphrodite, O, that's not PC,
we patronize thieves and lovers; now that's closer
        (and not without them do we desire
        or assume our changing what we are).
The language is changing again,
RU2 confusing any particular cluster
of familiar explanations?

We feel it, deep, like rain after midnight,
something there, so close, we listen
happy, feeling we'll be clearer
in a moment, awaken in a moment,
having slept dormant, as creatures
in forests through the dignity of long winter
become bright in the March chill.

You wake to more than airy images,
figures colored across the spectrum of dreams,
struggling, muddy footprints on their backs.
So, you pause a moment and wish for butterflies.

IX.

Words overlay, confront each other
then their sayer. A palimpsest becomes
a mind-map, words the computer's children,
seeming more like lichen on large stones,
melodic, readable only in emotion's grasp.

That's all it is.
Take a phrase and put it here, pick a line
And haul it over there, what sounds best
Sounds true, is.

Words search for freedom
in late autumn or early spring,
as blowsy thuggish flies batter
                windows stained with the exhaust of life.

                Bright letters of a child's blocks
                Banging haphazard on a hardwood floor
                Will make a word, but
                Turn another edge on another side,
                And again turn one block by one
                Turn a block again, and another
                Following each letter
                Take love, or war, or your name
                        (if you've blocks enough for that)
                A set of child's blocks will make a world
                Banging loudly on a hardwood floor.
Everything is language for us.
We become as a knot of words
shaken in a dice cup—we adapt,
we cobble, we shout, we scratch the wall;
a philosophy rises on each throw.

So, take back the first word into your mouth,
survey the dead on salt flats of memory
as the consummation of this abiding gift.

Each thing flickers but the last thing shines.
Each truth shadows   but the last truth between us
                              will not shadow.
Each is tangible in its own place
          though now a shadow staining the wall.

Gods humans mortals,
whatever we call these phantoms
of sand and air and desperate coupling,
whatever the translation,
the last shadow flickers in another's word.

Those words go where they will,
a spinning top weaves its way along
and betrayal is recognized, a costly moment
no matter the speaker, no matter the words.

          Then the vulture slides by,
a graceful shadow
at the edge of a blinking eye
with death
about to become individual,
a carrion dissolving
on the beak and talon of chaos.

Oh, you're so emotional!
          (I've been at this fifty years.
          Have I just this month
          Gone all mad and silly?)

X.

These slate grey juncos in early Spring
Scurry about dun stubble in wet garden beds
As eager to leave for cold pine forests
As an old man is to have bluebirds
Cardinals and gold finches buffing their feathers
For the spring show, coming slower
This year than last, and that year, then previously,
Or is it me he mumbles,
                                    forgetful
That spring, comes out of winter faster
Than his aching back now bends.

Consider the importance of birds
            They are the avatars of this electronic space
All these selves, the I and the you of them
Achieve, the same image within the interlocking rings

Of our biases, and flow-charts of our generations.

Behind us around us the wind will rise again.
We are alive in its presence.
We throw out our messages to whomever
Without our insistence might listen.
Our self returns through our cry,
As though our mothers called us in from play.
We balance, with the grace of folding hands,
This smile, the only vow that might be kept
For words are not enough, I tell you,
The best are bright translucent clusters,
Hanging like grapes behind those tender lips
That lilting Bacchus shapes into a smile.

XI.

I say you this poem after long confrontation,
and the meddlesome spawn of stories,
had driven through the shields and plumes
fronting my heroes wrath.   I am left to myself
in a minimal room,
                    a bare bulb burning,
                              the moon new.

The teachers like me, but fear dropped stitches
in the weaving response my mind portrays
when the eye flickers and mind must go alone
down projections of the empty places
in a geometry of wonder.

A point whose outside is the same as its inside?
I couldn't say that   at all.
How understand that separate language of perfection,
and its limitations?

But there was a girl....

She was petite, but had wide hips,
embroiled in myths.   Visions of Atlantis
are well set out and matched my dreams,
just the other side of a kiss.

Distortion embraced buildings, set them
swaying. Tentacles rounded fluted columns
on the city's heights.

Below, the phantasmagoria,
textured masses flailing, a color wheel
spinning to the grey of institution walls.
Feeding.

Adam me fecit. I don't believe it.
Who, then, tell me, tell me who am I?
...and you, why you, and you
are the name I had been looking for....

                I only remember fear I said,
the first girl, as dawn coming out of chaos,
when I learned how bloody I was. I. I. I.

How bloody it is to make an I.

(Holding hands by the lilac bush
I willed time to stop;
her father worked past five o'clock.

What a dawn! She did not know;
she did not know me, and I created her
with one eye brown and one green.
Her breasts were apples of the nine herbs charm.
She is the senses of summers past,
knotting my youth in sweetest pain.

Then, stolen by another in a golden chariot,
*   (a chopped and grey-primed Ford,*
*   fragrance lingered*
*   in the exhaust screen....)*

        Look back, remember, be glad,
recognize this bittersweet testament to youth.

Beginning and ending are chemical,
number, proportion.
Perhaps four octaves a throat holds.
A grunt a scream
—others,
others, gasping their fears in the eye's periphery
pretending interest outside the window.
Chemical… a last resort our genes bring through.

I do not know when I first went out
                                    to sit down alone
with the dice.
                          I still don't know,
            can't remember that.
But I have come through more changed
than I had ever thought could be.
Teachers look down, tilting heads and smiling.

XII.

After invention grapples with sunset,
rest the weighted shoulder's care,
the bound head, the chain's bruise.

I shall not invent myself things
and wrap them with tinsel
or dab red ochre in some sea cave
lit with phosphorescence.

I am through awaiting that muse
who separating sky and sea
rests a moment on the waves,

dancing. She is so lonely dancing,
dancing turns and clasps the wind
her hips have stirred,
and in her hands the cold serpent
of a tremulous fear is born.

Then, as she dances wild
wildly and wildly and…
coils enmesh the sacred limbs—
in the caress of the shifting wind
one's *Self Hurt* is born.

This creation, the palimpsest of fear,
clock and sun, is torn of this world,
abrupt divergent and laced
with the last dancer's bones.

All that is past: a web in the corner of a window-
pane reminds of a bridge against the sky
through the window of a speeding car—
artifice—
            of consciousness
bears this brutish imagining, what we did
before paralysis, and frames our minds
as a primitive halo on a painted board.

Always words demand,
amid whatever pain or lie,
the formation of a song.

Your body only from its angles
is the sentiency I give all for
in love 1000 times all different
yet the same woman

(She is he knows,
            the same as his 1000selves).

Light and shadow in curves of your body
 angles rounded of sharpness, of cities
  time is an island where the sea runs,
   songs abound your
    laughter is
     the sound where

                        Each day
                        Is warm
                        Where
                        Flesh blooms.

XIII.

...nevertheless—to name the colors in this fruit
one must have tasted,
even if the feasting was to touch in darkness
the brilliant yellows reds and greens
of the fruit and not the flesh beneath—enough
to inspire this distraction with desire
to have been touched
                              by time and flesh
& circle & kiss &   finite yet unbounded

Heads shaking. Heads shaking. Stand by me.

What is this airy thing we call a mind?
A bird moving through brush at the wood's edge?
Or caged, trained to say hello and curse?
Whenever you make a guess
it always rages, rages toward another
flesh and halting touches   the other
where actions converge to name only
slow processions under the sweet blossoms.

The long sweep of heroism takes hope in arms

*(in the wind filling spaces we become reality's dog,
taken wandering in the park
to sniff up the world and spray our mark)*

beneath dull February twigs;

adds new names to the implacable cells.
taut lines run from hard to hard in any life,
else how slip back with such vigor
after each forward lurch?   How? Why bother;
marking flags hint our proper boundaries?

(The myth loose in the factory/the die-maker at a loss:
What do they want up there–me to choose?)

Rampant fury demands all in an instant,
but we spend ourselves unconsciously roaming
the dark nights until that dawn we sense
we are not so favored as we were taught
in all the universes we face and face and...

XIV.

Each time I confront this place,
This attitude, a tidal marsh
In a recurring dream I don't direct,
I am more enraged. Will that ever stop?
I carry my skin, my muscle, bone, and nerve,
As a coat wrapping this cloud of mind.
Knowledge dissuades, belief justifies
This gibbering clown in the helix of it all—
Why chose to believe what we cannot know,
To cover this cluster of truth with grace and ease?

> *So, she golden wandering violet clouds*
> *a formless swirl— parturition sunrise*
> *forming Art mime's image my other—*
> *a brain trace firing magic combinations,*
> *a calcinate face behind beauty's reflection*
> *in eyes first shining, first calling it love,*
> *whose sockets darkened as this system spewed*
> *from whatever stuff we name*
> *this condensation of theories and close stars.*

It colors how much of the world we are.
We know it first our universe
Then it divides, the universe from us,
At first as other, my other when I,
I, stubby-handed, squeezed the moon.

Stories follow,
A handful of crystals from salt-flats,
Of the shallow encroaching sea,
Residue from time
Endlessly boiling the sea.
Stories, we learn,
Traveling in the sudden uproar of rare dreams;
Those that leave you shaken with your coffee.
Afraid to sleep again, but yearning to know
How they end. As we all are come
From some galactic night,
This right of passage is like lightning,
Forming the corona lucis round a smile,
     twinkling in mockery
     or crying surcease, please,
     I say, you say, can we agree—
     it will not happen before an untidy,
     wearing voyage?
  An hour might pass before we say

    Just let it go,
    we are weary.

XV.

Cronos' ruled: they are all gone now, do
their spirits survive   do

we seek live occasions   to enhance
the stories beyond such butchery?

Beyond imagination and our studious means
the continuous story rolls, beginnings fade

histories form as dust in raindrops
dreams refract from rainbows
and then the cold brings fog to morning,
refracting again until we become an infinity
of crossings, loves and grievances.

All our inversions recoil about themselves
endless revisions, revising as a magus
mumbling runes or calling the coin
for a lover's game of murmurs.
Chaos interweaves the grammar of our reaches
and the postcards of memory.

Did his words come from different thoughts
when he released her and laced his helmet down?
Or raised the glory of the living heart
above the feast of flesh and wine?

How can these recurring stories, though,
offer individual sanctuary? And do they?

What has really changed? Are we heroes
circling the rubble of memory's castles,
chasing our own mad curses,
suffering no more than infidels
throwing stones at Christian kings,
or verso?

Shall I choose the stronger God to make it safe for me?

Language moves me, moves multitudes and armies
against and through love balancing its sufficiency
on the dew-point before the fog of a morning,
navigating the void between our plots.

Given heroes and this new language of ours

> *(street-wise to language, rapping messages,*
> *neon rapture on the dark skies)*

I would kill these heroes in my choice of hour,
my scythe of words more treacherous,
my eyes cold as stone on a west-facing tor.

XVI.

to fashion what remains

buds are blown
without decision

dregs in the teacup
mold on the seawall
cities vined by garish flowers
the thin brown vein
in the porcelain cup

the gaze west and east
war or the mature
judgment of cowardice
the wen of the bullet
in the heart or the soul's heart

the mirror is the final tool and friends
reflect the fools within our selves

as personal these lines, *April the_____
missed lunch   had some coffee*

In these looming skies, now time,
well fallen on whatever was learned
is to be molded again.
All each followed in blood seems done,
modeled against the structural grace of years,
as the backbone of a striper, picked clean
by crabs in shallow water.

How random, one's dispositions in a week.
April paints the new leaves a joyous green,
(that green that makes the light seem lighter,
that green hidden in the gold)
          paints the names of all those things
tumbling in the pasture of our World.

Really, there is nothing, is there, to confess?
We flash as a beam of light bending
on the gravity of our circumstance,
straight to the need to repent what we imagine,
in just that time it takes us to imagine.

                    There is only the sea change,
                    the vulture's shadow sliding
                              over the meadow of a smile
                    on the silent arrangement of a face.

                    I stand   O   pageantry of it   O
                              the dirty movie, tensing
                    to linger in the basement of our arousal.

Do not, remember, do not
let sympathy over-reach your means.
It must be done in time, watching
the light fade among farther stars—
those same winking at you all night,
as the lights across the waters in Uskadar.

XVII.

That leafless day all plans fall off,
            as sand rubs the synapse of an instant
            and follows the winding surf,
            the skewed glances of unseen grotesques
            swimming in the hole of the ocean
            signals a size to disorder,
the moon in cold shadow,   the things, he

who in the meadow's grounded rainbow sees
            a surge of irony in glorious recession
            or in fantastic muteness enfolded in the shell
            on this edge of hours and moon-reckoned tides

who in shadows' perimeter chooses a minor conversation
            in light from the wine white as ice
            a trick is a trick, it works, it conjures feelings

who details moods the day nothing happened
            clear and warm when clouds caught fire
            and made you stand in the presence

(You returned to what had passed without a pause
to what was passing–the long loss–before your return)

who harvested the space birds had abandoned
            to store around this living heart

            breath turning frost on the windowpane,
seeing all sense lost in fragments,
those unique crystals
holding patterns on the screen of time.

Then as we fall into an echo—
which limns the beauty I have touched
and as I would act is led back
                    to acting thus–
Is it too much this mind survive?

Eventually

through briars and burnt grass
around a treadmill ending a maze
I would chew on seeds and claw the concrete walls.

When a sane man says,   "Well,
but what do you   propose?"
How respond to accidents on any journey?
What remains—*the mystic light*—
that glare
                    on the windshield,
            and the rush hour journey homeward?

(The play on the play's own tempo.)

Do what you must
Rain penetrates the dross
We leave behind.
That chill still eats my bones.

Would we believe those dead are happy
If we saw eternity before us;
Can this flower bloom, again?

Bending in wind and rain, glowing—
I scatter words, wildflower seeds
Over an un-mowed field.
I have grand visions
But I am only a jester humming.

XVIII.

i.
I say you this poem,
here there are more
than the two of us,
and thus, we must sacrifice;
the will surrounds as air
the flora, the fauna.

The path to confession has been for me
each step forward a circling, too,
a top spinning
along the high crown of a long road,
where the answer to all defeats
we abhor or worship as we will.

I am talking to a man, at first so senseless seeming,
another measure of the boundary curdling
my setting out, my stalking, my hunting and roaming
this vast country of unknowing…

> *…vast hall, marbled all around*
> *classical touches, pediments and such*
> *and the floor wild with hobby horses*
> *of every craftsmanship and art, ah glory,*
> *this bestiary of ideas, our only avenue away.*

Generations grow on their hardening pride
to disappoint us
acts we chose for them to mimic run askew
the fused bone of pride waives its rage
we look back through fog for good old days
rebuilding the lives we would not change.

ii.
It is two o'clock in the city
sirens are silent
windows open the first time in months
a mockingbird tests the air after rain
(full moon, high clouds)
shakes out his rusty songbook
on the edge of spring.
Thirty-seven songs in the heavy air.

I lie, shambling on the thin film of night…
He rests a time and sings again.

I wake suddenly at three am
shouting to myself, *Who are you?*
Watching myself smiling slip back into sleep,
my shout racing after—*Are you masque or me?*

At four am, still a fool, I find
words at the end of my fingers.
Stop you shrill coward—it cannot be,
I cannot know myself, I will,
to trace back toward splendor, try
again, then again
to make these uncertain confessions flow.

In this tactlessness, I have only
confessed what I could dream:
bringing down a ghastly cover

I hid in the pretension of darkness,
or hid in the clouds above her
as some others too,
for folly's learning was folly;
to bid a lover light is not discerning.

Yet, past an introduction,
or a separation, one must
go on, go on—*domani*...

XIX.

In living, there are seasons to be met
Hours to overcome and beyond, to envision a pact
With a year or an age—a pact with becoming,
Moments becoming successive moments…
At last, o recognize a life

I would live to sing you boldly enough
That our words become full lyrics
       our bodies the pipes and drums
       of a public melody, a chorus entrancing us.

Why, just the other morning, just the other decade
You whispered away my shyness with your smile,
Lying there in the unfurling light,
I over you, we captured the blossoming day.

Again, and always, the walls fall down,
Measure no longer exists,
We see our blinkered vision fail.
Around us, the sun rises, lighting
Our couch in this web of transformation—
Old love exfoliates our aging bodies
To the harmony of light and shadow
Over a deep sea that is some days calm.

Time, then, as I pass to electricity is
The sun's angle on the bloom, on the snow:
      this awe–
Each invents humanity, destroying
That single rage in each soul's crack.
I want your lust dissolved as a pearl
On the vinegar of my tongue.

XX.

Certain seasons we act as though
we would outgrow humanity
as though we might paint a world and go north,
armoured by words of glory and panache,
always searching an end of the wind.
Yet, there will be those who remained.
Save the gracious words for them.
Time then, we rovers dismiss, what cares
The light speeding a few miles more?
Who will tilt the gavel's empty judgment down?

Do not take that from us,

The stars drifting languid,
sometimes bursting
throughout our thoughts.

I have cast out a net of longing that all things
become the tactile freshness of my awareness,
cells of my palms remain on the braided rope,
my palms are polished as wood, gripping the gunwale.

Like morning rain   I   remember

                    and I remember

We fools walk numbers, to wrest a perfection
then trip over objects, all magical and random.

```
        O
       O O
      O O O
     O O O O
    O O O O O
```

TONOS WHICH HOLDS THINGS

Causeless animal, creatio continuo
1, 2, 3, between rock and psyche
find a key–we all sing, all must sing,
it is the defining talus.

At its base the soul rests, impatient.
Wondering at all this grandeur circling.

XXI.

Intimations in timid dreams,
laugh lady, love seems
constant as this present
shaking on ages. More
would come too costly,
a picture of sea, of shore,
with only the smell of dust
to fade the paint of Eva's lust.
Do you hear the blood in your ears?
It is the precipice where you leap
into your own scream.

I prepare my magic and my moment prepares
from winds from seas from nights—
a less poetic everyday, too real.

In that procession which does not end,
       wasted, not useless;
       to receive to take to die,
we are born, burdened, that hope
of some things we can never hope
will spare us sentiment.
There is beauty too in the consent of I
to the community of the symbol.
My place and its motion immeasurable
rekindles the birdsong where before
there were only shadows
and the darkening cloud of dying spirea.

The revocation of goodbye
on a summer or winter noon
teaches us solace:

solace can round us
in chords of an evening
when there is nothing spectacular
but the combinations
of evening; we look inward
or across each other's distance
to the lines beneath the eyes.

The last pose dropped
we begin to live without contrivance.
Seasonless, we are, we desire to be,
the question rests awhile.

XXII.

i.
Time aces me,
I have not seen the sea this year;
shall I explore the colored hills
or turn unbent and wander seaward?
It is the first of autumn but I
cannot see summer dying: old men
do not die thus   slate-sea
          warm into October, meadow fiery–
          a gold that dulls into dusk.
Old men drool out years
          wise old men/old maxims,
          words scuttle before crabbed hands.

It gets down to these passing daylight truths
we now must sit with in the dark.
I feel joint's pain and will not march again.
There's an emptiness I have not felt before,
Even when the vines went bare.

I fear death
          and you

you &   I
will touch a final touch.

For there is no trick here,
yet, a trick to keep hope living
is the trick that we do best.

Carry me, this will be all,
It is all I will be, the best
Of what I was.

Old maxims, how desperate;
we think we must explain.
Better, we just shut up
and let unraveling come.
Yet, I say it anyway,
for we each break down;
sometimes we are empty,
sometimes we weep.

ii.
Magic cast over love and evil
will come to the one who casts.
There is no choice of this or that
propels the humor, there is no this or that;
wherever we are this hour
there we chose again.

Winds scatters seed, I
shall make the field's hush a rune,
its touch– calling you.
       I have not lingered heart-parched,
each day drew figures on sand, until
I have drawn a circle where I live
and am able to say pretty spells
to guard this praise which is mine to you:

WHO SCOLDS   AWRY
BE MUTE
WHO SMILES
RISE HIGH IN
SUMMER NIGHTS

XXIII.

A river snakes
from the ice-cracked Pliocene
through the last bleached August day
to endlessness.

I have not seen this river real.
It is the river from the soul's longing
through the New World, another Fall,
the breaking wheel, splitting the drum–head,
through the last crush of each child's spirit.

This river is the story flowing, engaging
us with the blueprint from wild dreams.
This land's birth was an idea long hatching,
yet it burst like a new star bursting,
and we are the tic in a tic-toc too late.
So we inspect this claw in the gut
as though it may be other than hunger
for a past which never passed.

This river is washing away
the stone in the story anchoring our journey
as we wander between the poles of America,
finding the marrow of an Indian's bones
and tucked in silt, a piece of gold
minted in an imagined land and time.

So, there's the plot; fill in the blanks you see,
Find the stone in your heart.

XXIV.

America, museless, I am here again
Pausing to sing our names awhile.
We had a bluster of windy days on cornfields,
And space to make ideals to charm the world.
But like armies on mountains we grew
Boasting, without regard for consequence
And too soon dust
                              layered our fat images,
Towers of arrogance and honor
                                                    toppled down,
Becoming artifacts in the blue museum of deceit.

Because we need a muse, now,
With the ancient ways all gone,
We confuse youth with a soaring of eagles,
But no Metamorphoses occurs, no heroes call out.

Once words one spark
Across the black sky of mind
Turned a man to myth
Moonlike, waxing and waning

We have a wolf by his ear

The man soon gone the myth building among us.

No votes for freedom if no slavery
Bondage accompanies the one the other

And times will come again
When nothing will frighten the wolves.

Hypocrite and hero combine,
Show our humanity
How our world can diminish,
Red hair or green eyes
As certain combinations
Become clichés and clichés become the truth.

We all carry wolfsbane in a sack
Of enslaved lovers and family,

Except those with wide smiles,
Their eyes opaque as stones
On sculpted faces in ruins;
They always win, you know.
They never live, they never die.
They never know a Sally.

XXV.

America, you old companion, broken like me.
Voyageurs, we thought to reach somewhere else,
an elsewhere of heaven and earth meeting ideals
and the sweat salting fields under the sun,
a fulfillment, casual as lilacs, of the long poetic line.
Watching dreams dissolve
in the rented spaces of our lives;
becoming another bloody experiment.
Let us run from this hate and confusion,
or have we lost the gusto of it and the will?
Are we now to barter for a bit of quiet?
That cause of our self cursing
has been the same all days in all towns.
The tragedy was written, but on what?
How count the generations bearing our best thoughts?
Will suffering grow as remembrance recedes,
becomes more composed? Will words
ever work again to tell us what we meant?
Do I fashion only phrases, anxious to keep a meter?

There is a power here, blinded, flailing;
volatile alphabets are always turning.

Freedom is that mood of many strings
vibrating melodies beyond our hearing.
Something living may hear short bursts
or rhythms in the sphere of living blind.
Yet, history weighs heavy on the back
bent over a hoe,
                    hands weeding onions
on painful knees.

The pain will sometime touch too strong;
It seems so now ... the ancient dichotomy rehashed.
Isn't that the same old black, old white,
The old one-two, the new 0-1?

Between the stakes, we weave belief,
And we must choose better times ahead
From the awful objects which salt
the clouds of unknowing.

XXVI.

America, a river of continuous names—
the first river crossed, and we crossed it
with great loss, many men and always the women
with them, saying—
It is a dangerous game we play,
this freedom is an unsightly thing,
the mulch of pride, swallowing hopes
for finger breaking toil,
clenching stones until they yield bread.
But this pride, always fecund asks
what else shall we harvest?

—use the gun
to license all you wish, and wish for more—
more than that,
enough to say you've…

We can be as we imagine for
so short a season—hours
        even minutes count-up a life,
                        and we listen

WHEN THE HORN SOUNDS

beware
betrayed
the false jewelry
        elaborate lighting on the face
        the straight down
to which we thought we'd gone.

How could it last longer
than the summer dreams of children?
Why don't we give it up, then?
We never remember yesterday,
only the wishes we had yesterday.
Let's take all the pretty words and boil them,
make a soup of liberty, season it with honor
and simmer it with rage.
(If now I murmur Revolution, my friends smile.)
How did we get here (LOUDER) from there?
From that beginning, a marsh with no safe harbor
a primordial stench lifting
in garish light, bright green in the rotting air,
to this plot, nowhere left, this artificial smell
distilled from what belief said was to be.

How tell, how, again, in this lifetime
there can only be too many
of those we will not admit we do not know;
as for the rest– today, this hour, we know
as another love poem, an aspiration
the thing to rise, the thing to pray,
to sleep for, is not iconic as we were taught.
Then, say it as you can, say
the days are gone, I live knee deep
in the loss we gave this land
Where citizens begin to hate, then, hope again.

To forewarn,
                        there is a different sense
                        of getting through
                        you are not listening
                        to another's nightmare
                        in another season.

XXVII.

I build my garden in America, small penance
To ideals and presence. I feel now
I am enough along to look back,
                            cradle sadness
And give this confession of a small spirit,
Oh yes, small heart in the corner
                                against the gray wall.

I have found in words (small words,
                              simple syntax)
Staunching my portion of the rage
Gone viral across this hobbled land.

The spring is colder, longer,
And the rain continues—Mud *is*.
Seeds lay on the table, dormant.
The breeze stutters, turns around, in afternoon
Becomes a southeast wind bearing
Black skies and noisy rain
Cold as a politician's promise.

Put down those pictures you wish you were;
There is not grace enough.
Here is hope. Right here they say,
But tricked too often, some sense the scent
Of offal after slaughter, a tumult behind the wall.

Summer ends, somewhere always a summer ending,
Beating a refrain, our aging songs sing
Of soft edges on worn memories,

a proud presence at a revolution
holding one candle against fast winds
thousands in this army of youth pursuing visions;
ghost army in the valley of rejected prayers
marching through the hardened wax
to place a hundred candles against the fence of gold

Is to ride to the edge of our common self;
My moment too, but I did not know.
Where some will stand forever, preening,
Thinking their differences colossal
Saluting any error that will get though,
And others will see the beautiful indifference
And will smile years later at the beauty,
The energy illuminating all those rights;
Those whimsical heroes of youth.

Again in my old time, I believe in Revolution
Because I have no riches and I have no plan.
If I was betrayed by following laws
When the teachers shook their heads, or smiled,
I vaguely remember one, whose eyes were bright,
           whispered, smiling,

Carry a full curriculum, but major in revolution.

He was an amalgam of many I knew,
           contrite and uncontrolled, the descriptor;
Human was the word forgotten.


```
feed in at the first cell  of the stored
f sub routine, and follow instructions
```

        try to keep it bottled, hon–
    stay sane

XXVIII.

senses sharpen,
turning, the hill rises
up to a sky reigning blue
on fields of long grasses

where the battle dead
still speak through mist
to those lingering, asking
why youth was planted in that dirt
to grow such bounteous harvest,
lost in the drought of generations' self-regard
spreading a faint zone of memories
over the horizon, fading contrail in blue sky

tourists in yellow shorts are gone,
gone the bright summer spandex,
we are tourists,
with another season gone

we nail the open spaces and honors down,
these dead may rest until another summer

whatever we do
in September the world is ready to descend;
icy winds gather west of mountains

the light on stony places
            descends the hills
                        as though music resonating
                                    in this emptiness

sparrows are flocking
pheasants take the gun
the whole heavy-voweled harvest
in the cool-gold world

beautiful as the idea was,
the doom appeared
at its creation, its direction lost;
freedom's words will never end the sentence

as the creation grew a thought clung
like ivy on the oak—it must be true
failure's completion laves misery
on our families,
boundlessness consumes them,

hope poses in each; thought was freedom,
but they knew denial, and at first shocked,
they stared back nodded and shrugged
they could do nothing
in their snippet of this life,
but leap toward their lessons,
find that space too wide and drag
a net of moments back to hope
as dust in the diagonal light
of a yellow afternoon
catches the heart's attention,

a meager explanation
for these faces chosen to fill in
as mentors lost in pockets of the heart

XXIX.

I am   I am not   I am

                what will fire do

                only consume
                seem, should

speak of this as an offering
the offspring of wishes

given over from the womb
braggart beyond standing
to be pitied as a priest
without the touch of a god

the vast greed
            that surrounds us as bells
                        mourning in a country town

hysterical laughter
            in the next room

careens down exits
            from highways

back off   Jack

of memory, wherever it flows
a circle, outward   seeking
a river of the hidden
here begins that you
which is new to you

what is there I recast
to be said
(we make as a wish of numbers

our own magic spell;
they fashion well)
I desire to believe these keepers of tradition,
But the architecture has come up short,
Some beams are still attached, some arches hold,
But only the illusion of the plan, still abides.

Still, I might have escaped, been happy there.

The man who knows love feels its substance,
What it is made of. What is best
For his desires may annoy the still fire,
The long balance attacking the silence.

memories make us other people
lay down a memory today
on the same memory when you were different

So coming back to hide within myself, I bring
A bucket of words from my dubious expeditions.

A myth filler, paid
For leaving them
Their dreams,
Told to distribute wishes
From the well of hidden writing
To souls
Wandering in a forest of painted trees,

For the play must play…
                              you're in on it
your character waits for you

Break a leg in the Danse Macabre,
Play well, so drain emotion…

                    there's a drinking bout to come.

XXX.

i.
then: neon mosaic,
       don't forget pain
as a blunt wound
one is bound to declare
       beyond pleasure
       beyond blood's simple parts
       beyond this room's haunted eyes

golden strands   spun
sunlightsculpted
wistfulness

NOW GENTLEMEN

       drums   silver shimmers of cymbals
       a gown sways colors

       darting fish
       flashing in cold spring streams
       in sun-washed air

       receive the word
       birth from water

LET'S HEAR IT

       colors flash
       sounds caught and refined
       o rainbow

MISS   pure song name   sound
       whisper of precious metal
          polyvinylchloride
              sensuality grab-bag

ii.
this is the dance of time
our time, in which
the present is the future
the end of the end
the beginning-less end
the new time of light
the supreme time
        man, machine
        perfect symbiosis

when she rubs her image
against the light we are one
with the dust of the galaxy
at last our motion is uniform
she drops her dress
a galaxy is born

her limbs stretch
the millionmilemillion
sunspot tongues lick the void

all eyes reflect the light
percussing in tears of joy
        the lights swirl
        the music slows

the cosmos of her breasts
        is flexed unclothed

her stare is on Arcturus
she squats her sex exposed

iii.
then she goes on, the light of her eyes
hits in the room in the brain on the sun
eyes pale
all voyages are done

among the congregants
the skin tenses
each vies with imagination's jungle,
his own guerilla tactics;

who would be liberated with champagne
receives the false communion of soda
        (heat resonates organ like)
he has his accounts tomorrow

yet as he caresses the acetate
of her red dress
his hand
right comfortable and commodiously situate
he is the stain of love

(o drive away, familiar journey)
and all long journeys,
processed at the brain's base

iv.
Where you from, honey?
I come from outside
                        a small town.

each cell a time-bomb
laid in event's chain, detonated
          some night, bears prowl
                    in the scars of mountains,
an old man sucks his gums,
and his black lungs rip

the essential me flowing into my masks
small comforte that time helps fashion
beyond the face gorging
all faces that we are
a smile is forged
from being on the wrong street

(the mistaken incident
in the wrong genealogy)

changing every pattern
the journey becomes a new life
a log walk of the suicide
through the palimpsest of moments

v.
that is where it is done
in that touch–the Source–
from hypocrisy and the sham
of heaven collapsing on the earth
the Gehenna prepared for those
having hardihood
to make inquiry of such high matters
her sappho fingers do the rest

'the streets are paved with dreams'

o careless love, all eyes cast down

'whiskey and water' 'a beer'

the harbor awash/chart voyages

smell/love   quicksilver of women

medieval intensity: frantic prie-dieu
mannequins blessing
very rich hours very rich streets

                    vi.
entendre le grimoire
we hope for news
more potent than a thousand men
released to slaughter their brothers

gone in a howl of their adrenaline
out-speeding the clock, spanning–
the ardor of a universe without objects–
the history of the world crashing on a pillow

as a city too must be so personal, twist
the tongue and name each one, cartoon
of all cities–essential desperation
horizons unvoiced until the siren wails
consummation in the blood fire arc

cold metal
and the epical tolerance of plastic

vii.
The night is done is done,
the barker darkens the marquee
on a beggar framed in the doorway

above, the lunette of enameled glass
gives no reflection on the street

his monumental mass
still holds the grace of the child
and the reptile. After
long hours   he too will sleep,
for the music never troubles him.

me, Imagonna get me some likker,
maybe a gal named Sookie,
and hope for the best.

                    viii.
Walk the streets in a city, then wonder
How does it come to this, in all the cities?
The rambling agendas conspire,
Courtesy a crabbed knight's notion
And a banner left somewhere else.

Walk quickly eyes grounded,
Avoid the stroller on the left
Talking to something in the void.

Wishes are not enough;
What is it will unlatch the anger
That sticks on next door's barking dog,

The motorcycles' roar
Under that fellow yearning for heroes,
The freckle-nosed young girl, inked
Back to chest in red and green,
Like a canker on a plant that won't bear fruit,
But pleading for a glance.

…we no longer sing sweetly

The dancers are gone
and beyond, to each new season
our love seeks
in knowing itself
to be burnished
as natural objects
in the wind and lightning
of our thoughts
as we reach the stillness
                of each dawn

XXXI.

i.

now here it is, the best we know;
how imagination's seed created hell
and how our creeds trip over flesh
watch acid limning air,
etching freedom's limits

watch the news, its evening,
snatch the replayed instances of war
it's real, we're to the good shots now
it's real, we're to the dark times now

this is that year it all went bad

steps down from the pretty
'blood' spackled images
into the dusk of exhaustion
got us nowhere but through
certain times

                    which, not laughable
now cloy

sunlight, leaf-filtered
on the physics book,

                    we read
under the magnolia, in the quad,

not laughable but useless
after the long winter of Russian authors

a sense of the wrong road
more time gone, another bridge
flooded out with images of days askew

they needed to get through
those times as I these, and they
will not give aid to this useless formulary,
this cozened medieval script

61

1. Radiance of a swan, lingers in the abolished eye
2. Statistics of a constellation
3. Wings beneath the heel
4. Reagents of this orgy's bloody formulary
5. Shadows on dirty sheets

who warrants the coolness of this terror
not going to one's private place
one's hell at the bottom
of the cocktail hour, shouting

Stop that Man!

rather knowing in this lesser communion,
belief, as the sweat ring of the gin glass,
          is irredeemable–to be wiped away

clenched teeth surround the last metaphor

words will not form, hope's shadows,
they clutch the throat, were struck
to fete the heart's change

ii.
          let us talk
          quest became hope of quest
          humorous in retelling
          the end became hope of an end
          a pause, for an ending

1. Flowers imagined were metaphors of themselves.
2. Dried flowers, passed hand on hand, amid thieves
   singing their twilight songs.
3. Wings dissolve in the prayer's teeth at the mouth
   of morning.
4. Frail images in the meadow from a forgotten novel.
5. Behemoth cinema heads;
   > lead us, out of darkness,
   > genitals aglow, phantasm of dreams
   > lead us in tears, beloved.
   > The Exits are red.

iii.
beryl and foam arc
the marble quay

another port where the thief
lies blue-lipped under the streetlight
fingers flexing fingers on the railing
where dark thoughts strain the balustrade

a walker's shadow bends around the tree
as a creator descends to the garden

iv.
the automobile which may have hit you
had I not been there early

the automobile which may have hit her
had he not been there   or had I not
left keys in my other pocket and started late

v.
a terror of situations
lost in the general routine
waiting for some answer
by someone else to another's question

remember one breath in the dawn shadows
your eyes in the depths of flowers
when breath followed as a prophecy
to a private instant
with my touch following

counter to the clock face
o say a grace before your meat
or charred bones and ashes is all you'll eat

cutpurse violated and dreadfully ill
lace the street

artists paint boots
on lovers' faces
autogenously in blood

read their desires
taste rogue laughter
of all these souls

wrap them up
in a winding sheet

XXXII.

i.
We are all of us born of war.
                        Born of war.
There is no flight from that recurring game
As the winds from the West prevail, go East,
And further East until they are West once more.
What's it for, these killing winds,
These widening currents, all furious,
Conduct the meme of terror, become support,
All in the minds of all.

The toll-collector's back again,
            no longer
                        the heady names
                        no glory persists,
            no stalwart pose will win.

Each fallen from the web
Of home and family is named: Hero.

Granite, brass song, and holidays
Will carry all the dead boys along.
The frozen expressions
Neglect the strings of the possible,
The threads that would have been.

The days of grace are numbers,
A case of wide opinion and disgrace.

ii.
Now is My Lai or any pun of shame
Marathon Hastings Ypres lovely sounds, listen

[There's my Gettysburg home, then Antietam
Too too bloody I too had a brother, he died.]

Bring on more, all teeth in the warriors' smile
Let's shoot them in Babylon
Our marines are 'taking out the garbage'.

Some future still lodges wounded in the mind.
All the things we read they do in hell
We've made for today we do right now.
If you aren't right here you know,
Do it during dinner, watch the news.

Salamis   Cannae   Actium   Verdun pretty music,
Melodies, pretty words changed us most,
Still repeat; new generation's loves renew the loss.

Ask lovers of the dead the alley's name
Or the stream or the field without shelter
Where their boy fell,
Cut, slashed, stoned or torched.

Words polish the past, shiny enough for us
To keep walking west of the sun.

I can't stop now to watch the news
To see the stocks the weather and the war.
I can't accept how much I know
About the *danse macabre* of all this stylish flesh
A gothic style tints total madness now.

How did we think to pass unharrowed?

"It's all a pack of lies, you guys."

This is something fools surmise.
Guess what?   I'm one.

Mad once more, Madam,
And it's only two o'clock.

iii.

Now here is war—you're in the city, hell
Is total saturation, watch the news.
There is no way out, here, now,
There is no way to war on war, its fixed,
No surrender of flesh to flesh, for flesh
Is tainted, its for our will to know.

iv.

because it is____ what it is
give it meaning, give it balance
talk your book, at least
entertain us, freedom is gone,

                              limits of blood & bone
gone, too   death says

Party On!

             our bodies inflections
sweating, plane-eyed resort
whirlpool and lung-sucked
             silence

now ha ha ha hell is war
you touch TV's pixilated flesh

watch the news
there are no friends
             here or now
the electric pulse feeds the fire
pattern is the limit of desire

XXXIII.

i.

I have played with a muse
And been punished with silence
Until I gave over fear,
When luck, no reason, I knew
The ending of silence
Would bring another silence
Nurtured and raised
On its own infatuation.

Often this poem hangs off me like a ratty scarf
Too worn to warm, too torn to stop the wind,
A screed of rough weave, pattern faded,
Arranging the world to mirror the passion of the day.
Rarely do we say to lovers, youth grows on and on
And finally aged, becomes the relished pattern.
Love for a unique you in a special hour
Disappears as clouds might cover stars,
Or anger pull the curtain on other nights
As we rearrange the lights to staunch our needs
In patterns of the world wrapped
In curiosity and bloody scarred persistence.

My muse is moody, mystical and morose,
Today a whiny hag, yesterday somber,
A woman full of cares for all.
But it's tomorrow where I wait
For the brazen bawdy girl, wild-haired
Thin-ankled, bosom heaving
Til my eyelids tremble…

ii.

IS, that is =

To exist

It seems a foreign language
sea foam spinning from moist lips
je t'aime

exploding exploding a roar through the eons
is that it?

—to exist
a slang phrase in a strange language

Words block the rage
Some become fulfilled and see no future
In the striving of the seasons.
There the changes do not contain tomorrows,
Only missteps yesterday to the pain of today.
A few days slip through the cordon that pickets time,
The secret is a black space where words explode.
Their flashing blinds my anger at the day.

Hear the diesel horns haunting morning meeting night,
Rumbling on the tracks. Some early bird answers
From the acanthus in the alley.
The secret is buried, I feel it deep now,
Spreading across continents of the brain, turning
Muses into magpies, still passing a mirror's test.
Who were these daughters, these parents, who abides—

Now their previous eloquence
Remains in birds, their strident chattering
Their zeal for speaking truth and gossip.
The muse confounds.

iii.

yet   no storm   tonight
Chesapeake the Sound lights of Stamboul
orange peels floating in green water
past the Rialto's tidal beat
variation   everywhere I am
                    IS
world of the senses   remembering
formalized in the body   the universe
becoming   a response

Touch her touch her

        I reach through
The sfumato of the music
Gestures lessen
But ambiguity of the sweet vowels dancing
Round the clanging consonants is little comfort….
                    Instance beyond the instant
Nourish as system among systems
Growing toward the will
Spirit freed to chill exaltation,
Face to the wind, the sentence lost to air,
Misbegotten, we are lost to this good place.

Will it never end
This love I cannot stand
To trace again and again
The obsession of this thought,
Yearning when winter's blood courses
Round our shivering flesh and bones
For the summers of memory,
This child chasing the sound
Of crickets in the high grass of summer.

XXXIV.

Wild horses in my heart I sometimes will
when my weak-eyed, lung-seared rhythms
go one line.
So, guided by adrenaline's churning
to the heartbeat of a frantic time
like aphasic promises, like old king's rights,
I will to will what heart is left unyoked,
mine to do at least precisely what it does

to reinvent this elemental song, to witness—
nothing more—yet witness the magic of words
embedded in a perception of time.

If as a giver of laws, a listener to melodies
the I and a you, create a cloak of elaborate feeling,
a poem:Imagine, this smooth grey stone,
a relic, a tone of other times, found
after a heaving winter,
after a wet spring,
by the girl with long hair running
along the plowed field.
Each abides the laws,
the paths edging plowed fields.
And You—mysterious,

                      as though the thread,
the I attached to now

                    by this smooth grey stone.

And if it is hafted to become a stone ax once again,
dropped to search
the bottom of green water
for strings of the world to make an image.
What then?

Burnt round, ashes of the spirit.
Is this a time of high romance,
Or a misreading on the waterfront–

Understand, these are my friends
Swaying on the lips of disaster
Confiding soul to soul, human souls.

Shall we fearing afternoon, welcoming liquor,
Plunging to night, say, yea, mercy?

XXXV.

I see Leonardo's faces in the crowded crossroads
from the black centers of veined eyes
those wrecks hidden from another
all know their own opaque joys

what the I learns from you, sees in itself
we fear to tell, and secret grief extends
to gaze a middle distance

and becomes her body's experience
each incident a point in the portrait
becoming her self at that lush place
just beyond the timbre of her voice
a sand line at the bottom of waters
moved by the tides or ancient crossing
of storied lights in the blasting universe

to call this   ACT   living or dying
an eternal memory
of tomorrow the omega of her feeling
then go back to the alpha of morning
varnish this portrait,
use resins from vanished forests

let love explain itself, call out
objects in each remembrance as fire
glistens at the gate of winter
and each kiss lingers in memory's poison

as if we found photographs of Helen
in the deserts of Egypt
where the grass, rank spring life,
left, parched earth sounding
to the step all cry: water, life

love explaining its gross turnings
always approaching, growing, circling

I have found myself out-
out-tricking the muse
was another projection   of me to you
and love ending
because of the impossible
reconciliation of self
among all selves
as the muse celebrates the barbaric yell:

we are inseparable, isolated in odd moments,
            inventing this muse, an excuse
            to throw words at the sky
and hope some return in an order we can bear

The surfaces of all bodies
continually emit radiant energy.
They will radiate their internal energy
to a temperature of absolute zero;
the universe will be dark and cool,
as analogous as mass over light.

entendre le grimoire news at the hour
chimes, chimes, chimes, beloved
            eyes changing shape
skin and hair and bones of your fingers
we are fading into the resources of our grief

XXXVI.

To remember last spring's flowers
to sing Kyrie among the red-cheeked
under bright marquees hovering over the streets
ashes drift unseen in weary evening air,
as the juggler tosses his bowls to stars.

In each year's reworking,
presentation becomes arbitrary
beyond meaning, becomes definitions
of self—the air, our breath, in its turn,
dissolves our position in the images

others reflect in our eyes
and our applause of the defeat
of that which we were said to face
so bravely, juggling those bowls
heavy with life's embers glowing.

These fingers stretching, reach out,
at least we make valiant efforts to survive,
escaping hopes and memories, to arrive
in the daydreams where we live.

Birds are wishes pinioned on the sky.
Our blood courses free, you—
hold my day bright brutal and silent now.

XXXVII.

Wish Justice to the living,
how wrong we often are,
how it often becomes
too transparent to abide.

Each place we go I set roots
from stones of fruit fallen from a bird's note.

I can't remember there or here,
now, I remember crows left holes
in half the fruit, oxidized
as blood around a gut-shot.

I own a need to have been somewhere,
chance seed bearing slight,
as was its chance, fruit; sour,
crow's meat, a haunting past,
an orchard, a life, trivial,
but the stone of the fruit grounded.

Light spills over from the solstice,
the shrapnel of a story,
a bygone farm on a stony hill,
the dark missile of the hawk's shadow
crossing the orchard, to perch high
in the walnut tree
edging the pasture,
admirable, alone,
          a stone carved in a moment,
          before his trajectory took the mountain.
He left me his talon's shadow
deep in my thoughts and wonder.

Once dusk froze so quickly into night
coming over the pasture
the snow crust knifed my ankles bloody.

One day the day itself was frozen,
even the pheasants were slow
to explode into the white squall.

I held awhile, but this was not home.
I lost the movies of those orchard battles.

The web of seed and nutrient,
endless seeds of body spilling
on the battlefield extended from the mind
in the occasions sponsored by remorse.

Which seed was taken of all
I had to give, one with worlds
not yet known

                —to weave this private life
called, I'll play your game?

        Variorum of Survival's juices.

So, hawk, I, talons

                in your white flesh
sink myself

          into your blue veins.

XXXVIII.

i.
I'm old, annoyed, but dogs still bark
beside the Jezreel wall. Seek
down the days' shifting chain
to walk in the park when workdays end.

We go on because of details
we get hungry another hour passes
there is laughter there is a flower
we are too tired the motion is onward
we cannot pull back the days repeat
there is the physical molding of time
into the deepest of feelings.

Like love like hate a longer time
may create forgiveness.
Be lost, then, forgive—
bear forgiveness
like ripened fruit.

As our illusions crumbling streets
turn to ancient alleyways,
our legions maul the tribes
that did not cross borders
as we did once
now some hold out one hand
for bread and lift the other in a fist
demanding to be as we.

In the fullness that comes
                              for all,
I too, took hate into my life
an exotic pet, a choice
of seekers who walk in city parks.

ii.
Even the closest are gifted a rage
When various details of the self
Clash with those of the other
Before a dinner or in a company
We need to acknowledge.

Then loath the crone
Covered in soft screeds,
Gnarled fingers glistening
Reds and blues
Of costly jewels,
The false clarity
Of diamonds,
Who commands love
And dispenses her tithe of hurt
Down the aging years—
All these mysteries
A muse might play.

I should be wise, I have thought
Enough and deep
As my mind allows,
And call it capable or not
I bored deep into my own fears,
But what is deep
In this world merely stains another.

XXXIX.

i.
I am in another world right here, a diatom
On a glass plate—all our brilliance
Polishing—dust motes in the afternoon
Pales, I know this, tell you now, pales
When it is all added up and you laugh
Not at cynical accounting—laugh your laugh
Of sudden surprise.

Masks no longer hold our newer secrets.
We build our avatars spinning
In the dark matter of communal secrets.

Time is the only sequence in a life
The other fears. Even though smiles pop up
And reason searches answers
To hide a ration before the coming hunger.
It's a comedy, but these vestiges lead to something dark,
Like creatures without expression, facing pain.

I can't say it comes before or after
But feel there is more now,
To wear down and break the green world,
The thriving air of flying things:
Gnats in the light, stars after.

Every generation reports worse times to the next.
All the times before had this or that as jewels,
But time cycles itself, becomes old
And passes that phoenix torch along;
Each birth loses, curtains fall, each hero lies down.

ii.
Who would cast beauty from his own form
approaches the end of the spiral,
flesh touched into an image,
firelight, chants in the dusk as a foreign tongue,
in seed through act to child
          shoot roots from the spiral.

From shepherds, conquerors,
the iron wheel bites, beast again,
to kill all but the imitation of the dance.

Walking beside you—
in the act is the pace,
an accumulating, a residue of each day
each brilliant error towards a knowledge.

XL.

Our own eternity away, a star tips its light
in the eye, light in the gin,
drink it in and in and in and in,
a kite of subjectivity lofted–
a prayer-like wish from the heart—

love as shattering
as a hammer on a crystal watch-face.

There is the art of the egotist watching
mind pleasure itself as though a body
lofted to some apotheosis where all
gods enervate. In the rhythms of objectivity;
this silly fool desires to sustain this motion
a moment with no surfaces reflecting;
dying inside, this headless snake in a sunny hour,
as everything is seen after the fifth martini.

...and how to meet the mortgage–

ii.
the city still covered in a smog
of sickness madness and bad weather

–wish we could get
to the farm–if not for me for the baby's sake...
*   lack of time I bewail is really my own fault,*
the students are not demanding, but each time
I would sit down to work I turn sleepy,
stay up most of the night with insomnia
(the many colored straitjacket of our neuroses)

finished third mystery novel of the week

12/7–dinner at parents   *they age*

searching for the one thing different in the library
the last of the snow melts, afternoon turns balmy
trying to cross the street at five o'clock

what I was, what I am about
having lost   interest in the profundity
of galaxies   long after their light
was hedged with bets on love
lost hard   spring and green
are for the species   I light a cigarette
and ask you will you give   if I do

then, looking out a window at rush hour,
we think how alike earth's, these demons in the air–
the glow of sleep is a terror fleshed;
hints now reach from higher chemistries
painting a smile of malice on a face of a god

nothing beyond
the malice which sustains like grain
the tumbling generations
the children of lust
bred for the slaughter and the art

iii.
Ask who must die that this foundation rise
on whom will the mark be made
to dress the stones and lay the walls?
There will be none left to prepare the earth
for seeding,
the wedding of season and mind.
There will be no feast of spring, no harvest home
only memory of that feast on the lips
of the old, the stories they were told
of thread worn images on faded cloth.

Some say everything is dim, not to be descried;
we all live in a book
trying to find our names and what we did.

iv.
Above the city a brown fog drifts to the streets—
particulates, the ashes of deeds, geometry
of an Apocalypse, where the stare focuses.

legend no, this living warmth
the steam of ghosts enfolding
torrents of words

from desire to memory
to touch,
o, that's a long hard way for words
like meaning hunting the egg of the universe

our names will not change, but each
becomes other through aging's uneven passages

until one says, 'You still look the same
after all these years.'

seeing only the you that was
once

XLI.

IMAGO HOMINIS
Think about nat of un nature of universe and same
time ah what time now woe-man think of
woman/manglory rational but must   be best
          insignificant not a sign of him away– out
there/proof of the exist of go(o)d

Infinity is
8 gone low_____Time equal duration of awareness

Time in space_____capability
So fragile/must imagine   structure
     value
          Nat of gud simp
Too, emotion/seems   upward of reason
                                   Cant control it

               Light creates   Opposite of space

Alone in the honest terror of the wind
I wonder why I attempt to stand tall
when each new sentence begins from this wonder.
Yet, wherever it goes it ends at my feet

like a pebble in a puddle, or my marrote lost
in the summer life of weeds.

sklerá(fem.)   Hard sclerotomy

I will still see
a thing, an it of many hands
boohoo everything, separate
waaah of self
                'a conscious part of the conscious
whole–which relates only to other parts 2 offical
is larger than 5 more shoes more chocolate
o what a wonder
they were the enemy and just people
therblig our thiasus
and by frequent songs
set her on the lips of all men
she's the one gets me through
this addiction to patterns this jester's tongue
my words fall off

                        do it do it

      machine goona get me machinegonna get me
                machinegonnaget me

              shall I strive to an heavenly joy
                    with an earthly love
                      Adjectives of eyes
                      Noun verb noun
                     Noun copula noun
                           Noun
                         Syllable
                       .,?!,. breath
                           Tone
                            ?*?
                            ?*?
                            ?*?
                           turn

On each living arc, time quickens
senses alert, is this love, breathing in
     the shadows of our daily needs?

Time is a flower blooming,
beckoning a cradle of space,
pebbles smoothed into meaning
by the vast river's past majesty.
The ocean of symbol and dream
framing itself along a beach
in a windstorm, the sting of words
unfolds meaning like a pall of clouds.

XLII.

i.
I tell you the moment I became divine:
When in the instant of dawn
Light appears a grey cat on the windowsill,
Prowling forward, growing out of darkness
Suggesting that darkness is not absolute
And the winter's images of morning
Top and bottom are contortions imagined.

The importance is—the simmering images
Loaded in a series I could find rest in;

The instant I made a road of words
You could dance down to your home,
You too became a deity in my mind.
Will I be the same in yours?

The power to see it all is there
On the wet jiggy sponge behind eyes,
Awareness filters a singular pattern

Of words to meet interests outside our ken:
A dark wood engulfed in radiance.

Acceptance waits, confined until
Those scattered times light touches
Within the leaky sack of our imaginations
An incoming tide, and the heron turns blue,
Those times when immensity is felt as nearly here.

In these deep nights when I am not
As old as I am used to being,
Woods are quiet, owl notes distant.
I am quiet sensing the world willing
To send me answers to wonders
I formulate on wordless nerves,

Reveries stretched so taut by yearning
I forget where yearning began.

I think I'm not afraid now
Those are the few good nights
Sometimes the effort is as counting stars
The worry can goad one to excess,
And knowing our frailty, how little it takes—
Such a tiny distance from where we live.

Blank depths of the sea, cloud scud with birds
Where energy escapes the picture and the mind.

That time of night when clocks go dormant
Because dreams don't care for clocks, and you
Smile that chase me smile, and disappear
Beyond the lost wail of the black train's horn
Leaving me to turn and clutch the blanket's lost
colors,
Opening my eyes. the dark a little lighter,
promising
A feeling, a something I cannot see.

ii.
When we don't know who it is,
This other we thought to know so well
            we might stand alone and realize
            we knew all along the feelings
            we wished for
            we had gathered in a cloth
            which had frayed.
When I wake each night, age brings
Worries I would not account in earlier days,
            Petty obsessions grown to giants.

Instances forgotten in the light
Slither through the hours
From one awakening to the next.

Occasionally, some night waking
Thought remains
Stuck in consciousness,
A splinter in a callused hand,

Visible but not painful. These are thoughts
We think of as the detritus of sleep.
I wonder when dreams seem like gifts
And waking a loss we must endure.

I measure time in short then shorter blocks
Because intensity keeps rising and resolutions
Are broken so quickly there are days
When I rewrite a resolution for tomorrow
And hope it stretches past its inception yesterday.

Today, snow is dusting us, not enough
To think of ice ages and before,
Although, here we are, it is cold.
There are no dinosaurs, only shadows
At the back of the room
Running through the day
As the changes include rain,
Then the sun tries a streaky wink at dusk.

When cold mornings make me yearn for fire
A place to sit and conjure my portion from myth
Waiting for heat can make a day long
But there are vast deserts to invent and air
Shimmering with apparitions clothed in fiery deeds
To wrap these dreams in words.

iii.

Hours are few the nights angels visit.
I may be king of all I dream and dream
Someone I do not know invokes my dream
Call them muses, whatever needs we collect
From those who share those traits,
So many have gone along the fence-line wondering
How they too must recall the thoughts of all
The featureless shuffling on this dusty path.

Muses transform from secret parts of mind
Muses might be wrong, misleading,
Our sins only instances of our mediocrity.

When the face of the muse who tricked us
Has added from Memory, and waiting
Has become the new game on a new night

That stands solid as elements of waking
Earth, sky and wavering tides,
For myself a hope persists even now.

For others I cannot judge I cannot tell.

iv.
Collage of words fleshy as ripe fruit
Collage of words robust and bursting
Like flesh of plums

Filling again with gods moving over forests
Mountains made sacred with hidden altars
A world tumultuous, spilling on my eyes
Gazing at a wall close enough to touch
And dusk settling all over my window

I keep shuffling words across the page
Waiting for voyages in my awareness
A glitch in my focus, a misspelling
That leads to meaning

Ice comes skimming puddles in the park
A reminder of something as I walk
Each morning, trying to loosen my knotted legs
This cold season bears down on me
Pushing me towards the infant I once was.

XLIII.   IN A GARDEN

i.
The sun fires stripped woods in the March dusk.
Out of the burning this old man mistakes the breeze
For laughter, replies his own HA HA and trembles.

"Once again you come too early,
Catching my unwary eye with terrible light."

I stand in the garden and remember, often.
A bouquet of faces, as leaves change seasons,
Will flash among the flowers
Telling me of different times
Condensing long years into instants
Of ripeness.

So, I am alone in muddy boots, listening
As the birds tattoo patterns on silence.
The notes of various songs burnish the mind,
As staring at stars the night of a new moon, the eye.

March passes, but winter won't
Instead, it mimics the betrayal
Of hope that is the loser's course
In the ending of a love affair.

I go to the garden these mornings, hopeful.
The wish, for a good day for drilling seed
Misleads without a miss, all my garden springs.

I am bewitched each April wanting warmth,
Knowing too, there is a counting,
A number attached to my coming Aprils.

And bewitched again because
Knowing the complete sequence,
Particular emotion, ending back to belief
Without the language, knowing
The fullness swelling consciousness,
I become more innocent.
I believe now, now it is too late
The order was to tend the garden,
That was all.
The me of that distant past, that youth
Of brash whimsy
Did not suppose the order elegant enough.
Now I, old, contemplate invention sprouting
Gracious worlds from a few rows of thin soil.

Some of god's fools build gardens as a refuge
For their better thoughts. I do, for my few ideas'
Attendance not to wither
                              in this shallow particular soil.

Then, stand in the garden and live again
The impossible coil of all your lives,
Possible in the length of a breath.
Become a mathematician to follow equations
Of the lives of all you might become.

ii.
When I stand in the mud of an April garden,
When the rains continue and the cold lives on,
I think of trouble down the lane and up the road.
There is no Muse telling me to go inside
And write words to circle my doubts;
Thoughts are cloistered here from chaos.

Splendid and rare the ideas opening
To those on the high-wire between events
They thought led from an instant
Toward one expecting like seeds, Spring.

How difficult to collect water and attend the season?
The growth takes nothing from you
Only your unbent knee and your pride.
Caught in the culture of this morning
Is not a retribution;
As each inheritor needs shoulder the sins of parents,
This holy landscape dies in a geological moment
Since the melting ice began to host the life crossing.
Some made it, outside the shadows of beliefs
And they thought their gods pleased,
And the carnival barker's imperious shrillness
All came down to not attending the weather.

XLIV.

i.
Listen, a small part of this, gleaning…
A mottled fruit on a withering twig,
Results from the implacable world haunted
By bright green monsters.

All seem small in these multitudes,
A deeper garden of sex and death manifests
In mud or parched dirt, it makes no difference,
A bounty will engorge the land again some year.
It makes no difference, your harvest's failure.

*"If it don't stop rainin soon, those skeetters
gonna be bigger'n blackbirds when it does."*

Plant an elderberry at the garden's end
        Where it turns to marsh,
        Where the swamp magnolia
            scents the air
      And turtles flash
            orange embroidered shells
Bright in the warming day.

Take your notes for living off the grid,
They cannot take your freedom
If they don't know you have it.
Flowers are fed with the blood of saints
And the blood too of murderers
They do not distinguish and take what they need.
Strike back when you can.
Remember this rede from the elder
      Twisted to today

AN IT CAUSE HARM, DO WHAT YOU MUST

Me, I want to beat birds to the berries.

96

ii.
A dawn breaks when there is only growing old to do
However we have aged,
we still tote books of memories to guide us,
depending on the hour we choose a book
we take our coffee too hot
then sip it slowly as the shadows move
and wander in this library of faded deeds.

Sometimes remembering the season too,
sometimes only a city, a dock,
or aged buildings on a sepia colored street.

Perhaps this poem will end before I
simply let it go—
the world could end I see this morning;

entertain us, freedom is gone, limits
of blood and bone gone, too

—never try this at midday, memories are all bereft...
choose the morning, the fresh chill
or afternoon warmed as the blood of youth
assuages the stunned awareness your eyes record

Memory I know; no, it is gone,
the hope I had to make myself

seem prescient and even more
someone who made the good moves in life.

iii.

I hoped to justify myself to self.
But look at me—it didn't happen.
I always spun the poet's words
after the instant passed,
and she had gone. Over the left shoulder
a certain dream followed, formed
from the low of maybe, the mist of why.
In the real heart's time
I stuttered across each present instance
palms sweaty, neck flushed, word shy,
a babbling of shame and fear.

Capturing the words to match the faces
always the freshness of youth prevails
around each memory.
Now I look into the eyes of young women
but they don't look back.
They are always as fresh rain,
but it's a drier season now.

Perhaps there were grander wishes for us
for all, able enough, but disconcerted;
a bluebird hops in the sunned grass
eating those tiny dragons that would be butterflies;
the swallows weaving, protect the air.
We live in an agony of going away,
and give ourselves analogues of taking leave.

XLV.

i.
Beware your quick rebuttal
have a care, caution should circle
playing with the way your words should fall on air.
There are many I's in these words and several you's

1 kleptologue   *2 plagiarist of dictionaries*
                3 composer of Bedlam's song

in shadows of words love scampers,
a fractal of the life of a leaf;
notice, most of its year spent inert
laying on the earth.

Limits occur, short notice, no matter
what or how we care
when words are changed, does the story,
wrenched from its strong plot,
sluff off explanations leaving hesitation,
rumors, questions
to the spurious characters we project?

Many gods have ruptured the thin membrane
holding daily moments, holding us from flying—
this one from fiery woods
was a stripped down familiar, no white beard,
nothing but an imaginary voice,
out of sundown light, remembered
as an accent in a teeming city,
perhaps a deli counter accent shouting:

"Don't Ask!"

Each time I hear that now
grey cathedrals fall
altars shatter, I stand once more
in the instant dust of my rejections.
The voice from light is in me,
its fire a projection of my fear.

You could rebuke your own anger;
What would it cost you to wave it goodbye?
And could you pay? Meditate, count a smile
Across the table plated with hate?
I can't.
I grow old. I grow fractious.

ii.
Should you toy with my private shadows
My pens, my pages, my lucky stones and carvings
Then hear my curses like grapeshot
And sense my curses' spittle on the air.
As you move up the stem of my brain
Past the talons of dinosaurs and birds
You might find me some days in that spongy part
Where curses coalesce. Beware, they hurt
With a numbness which does not unwind
But stays the same, the same,
The pathetic lists of hopes grown old …
Will hit you as a flatland storm
Abrupt, implacable, and humbling—
The force of life circles like a moon.

Understanding little more
Than one understood before,
Not clear-headed, just feeling bad,
A freezing feeling in your head,
Remnants of ice in a deep past, intruding now.

XLVI.

So many people carrying lists.
There must be secret lists of what we miss.
They must be very long,
longer than a winter morning,
as sadness comes so easy, a natural way
to see the birds when green fills in the world,
and shortens our horizons,
focuses us on the garden bed before us.
We blame ourselves for every murder.
It should be like laughter, our pride's response.
On a bad day, stand in the garden,
watch the slayer and slayed,
and mind riddles out that almost everything
is out to take life from something else.
Murder in the garden is for the belly's sake
or to spread the spawn more cleanly.
Yet *we* murder best when our belly's full,
talking abstract visions, standing at the gate.

It's May
when the shoo-flies

rattle your brains.

The sense of peace leaches through tired limbs,
even the bones seem wobbly, the muscles unsecured
cooling in the shadows stretched toward evening
the breeze is from the south over water
birds are very busy, preparing for the night.
I have heard these songs so many times

emerge from cocoons of memory,
stories mostly indecipherable,
promises from a transient god.

XLVII.

Truth leaks little and little from the cracked drum
Of greed we run our engines on. Parents hurt
Little by little, the children too are listless,
And the old stare and curse more loudly
Those friends held sturdy by their illusions.
Greed is the infrastructure of these decades
The rusty bridges over the risks and rewards
Of living, and there on the grass a broken shell,
A wisp of straw. Remains of a nest
Tell a story wandering through deep-time.

So all those dead who lay between the rocks
And paint the black cliffs with whiffs
Of cirrus clouds on a day of shadowy light,
Hear the message from a deepening river.
Ah, these small clues to what went on before,
Unlocking small matters to what comes after
In our weak history brushing the land,
A short drizzle in a wet Spring
Tell there is no understanding what we do.
I've hit my limits and looking back
I'll be brave and shrug; I hit my limits early.

Tell me the world is falling down, an avalanche
Around what ever is standing now, but listen:
Age comes smiling—the past
Is where the future lies, and we invent the past.
Almost everything through deep-time's run
Has been held in the seductive maw
Of a quickening loss—long stress/quick shock,
The reef-gap after extinction.

Leave stones where earth's continuing ruckus chooses,
And leave bones of heroes where they found a home.

All relations will glance around,
The bickering in families cease.
First mother needs no other name,
The vague fathers are better off unquiet, anyway.

I slip through years, a salamander in wet grass
Disguised in colors of the world's necessity.

The sun is a baleful fire through the woods at dusk,

And I costumed in motley,
Dance on the arrows of time.

XLVIII.

i.
We spend ourselves carrying the possible
in one overflowing cup balancing on the world
until jostled into spilling the last dregs
of these improbable years
we gasp, holding life so gently and say—ah…
neither answer, question, nor excuse.
Whoever yells to us to obey the laws
is surely one whom pirates fancy,
cut-throats and brigands applaud,
and the small man with his collar up adores,
sidling the shady side of the street,
wishing to stand and yell without redress.

We try to obey what we hope
the laws at least might be;
if we could be as we would be:
but we mimic a scrawny bird,
broken-winged plucked featherless,
iridescent plumes layering the earth
like deeds forgotten,
even our poor children embattled,
slow surrendering to time,
the bones brittle, the smooth flesh tumbled.

Ah, what wrinkled and mottled stuff we are;
a grease stained and wrinkled shirt
at the foot of the bed.
                                        All to achieve
the certain knowledge that we don't
know much and what we do is mostly
useless, and any new understanding

    is   just   too   late.

ii.

Imagined harmonies drift off the compass
as glimmers from the last star
just arising at the end of the mind,
and we obey what we hope
those blood shuddering rules may be.
We are an aberration that took hold,
all incomplete, we grew a viral pride
that feeds on the world
a hope that a presence will come
to take us back
before pride was loosened
and began a world,
but it will not because
pride is the catalyst
in our being's strut;
we are not if it is not.

It is the acts not the book
cohere through all these words, like blood,
when for a little while we meet
the exigencies of day
and I say here is a song
and here I am worried about this
or that stupendous wrong.
        Is that what we are meant to do?
Strings of the necessary connect the lot
of what we can be, and the lot of all options.
Because the continuous takes as necessary
all the plots and their possibilities—
the happy outcome and the end
which separates the tear from the eye.
And if it drop, what then, this tear,
passing quickly, yet constant as the sea?

XLIX.

i.
In the postulates of love
lay the currents of both
the blood of our necessity
and the sea breathing tide
necessary and flowing homeward,
where tenderness and hatred etch
veins on static rock, painting the way
back on dark streets towards home,
past caverns of empty skulls
lapped in ebb tide, unlamented;
the king of changes dispenses justice here.

We dig cisterns everywhere
to save our dreams of rain.
Sometimes exhausted we turn,
ask was ever a city really here?
Will the burning reach 12 cubits down;
does the moon turn bloody in October?

in old books   on TV
or when
I lay me down to sleep

*[there is a fresh spore on the snow
something is in step with me]*

I pray my soul to keep
so words,
love's necessities, common as aging,
become
naming and remaining
they say your history is here
we read signs amid this loss

red lights flicker on astonished faces
we sit here
through the humid night
amid   the ambiance of bombing
caught between   concrete
and the hope in a leaf
searching all our systems
shielding tomorrow in a seed
          the language is an old variant
                    among disputed syntax
                         the accents live
somewhere among these lists

Who speaks?

the city the people
those walls mark a church
those stones were a steeple

this is the republic of dead men
have we among the living
a vote to cast for them

there is trauma in the thundering
shadows   wherever
homo erectus has been found—
this very long creation called a man

who prophesies
from the darkness of this night

arc of blade thrust of point
who is it cries
be still you make the stones shake

the hollow skulls still sing
we have fragments of arms
wonder in a bag of teeth

the scream recreated from long silences
louder from the depths of such silence
retreating into the silences
which were to come, are now still,
and yet to come
each silence is a body awaiting
the solid hurts that shadow
the mind   watching, averting
always back to learn it again
that firey creature wheeling through the mind
hear the dead, the extinct races, all those
held in the courtesies of a ceremonial time

as echoes from the stars

ii.
I look out and the rods and the cones of my eyes
gather light from plinths and palings of creation.
I know the vast unbound universe
licks my eyes, I gather silence.
This counts my knowledge purifying words
as those become a consciousness,
a final past dancing toward a final future.

Here is the meaning I have found
share it with me in the hope of finding grace.
But it is not free to any of us—we must each give
gold coins for our eyes—coins of the thought
that rests at the heart of our dreams
telling all we can know we already know,
ready to be released from inside the mind.
Beyond that we cannot search—
beyond the boundary
becoming malleable shifting on our approach
hanging a curtain of knowing
to block the suicidal track,
slick with generations of tears.

iii.

unneeded   unrequited a certain joy
makes noises and the noises cohere
patterns begin our hope
our reason to be
the five stopped flute of griffon vulture's bone,
an ivory figure still fertile in the clay
always breaks through to song,
but where is this past on a circle

awaiting a last song as each of us
has a last song to meld with the songs
which have gone before

from the first
each piped a singular melody; he's certain
she has added her own harmonic,
so the layers of the tune
seem the reachless background wave
of the galaxies' flight,
from the first piped melody
a note from each, their vibrations
filling lapses in these resolving harmonies
yet unheard.

L.

Each of us encompasses the other
either rising or falling, and the time
when a stasis can be felt one to the other
is the link which lets us know
that the loss is not the same loss
we had learned we thought,
but the casting aside of that sense
of belief in the loss,
            wishing for stories
without the intervening and useless time

                (as in a play between the gaze the kiss
                as the messenger arrives
                hoping the message uplifting
                a bright blade victorious).

We are born with that loss—
was, is and will be—
that survival MO—masks, money, morals
is not our plan—who would keep on
knowing what awaits
if it were not growing in our baser parts.
And then to learn, often at the worst time
that each lover is a self as adrift, as bereft as we.
What we counted on was hope in company
having confused the company as lover,
once, twice—for many a lifetime's search;
seeing at last, the company was all;
the hated the murderers the heroes of religion
the hypocrites of language,
and all the blind on pilgrimage.

Where was it though, and when
was betrayal recognized, that costly moment
when the crimson face of the vulture
floats gracefully by,
its shadow like the eye blinking,
like an angel muttering to death,
no syrinx, no song,
about to become a chaos,
already a carrion explored
on the beak and talon of life.

You, I, and someone over there
glance at clouds passing, make lists,
ink directions to hideaways on old brown maps,
hope we won't fall off somewhere,
imagining dragons at the end of oceans,
building a glance at the lacey world
decorating our list of memories
of what we had throughout the years
we thought we were growing wiser.

Who looks for laws affirms them.

LI.

i.
Muse of my spirit, you love, in the reaches of time,
Give spirit to our common words, flesh to spirit,
Spirit displaying the bloom of the flesh.
If there is 'purpose' it has no understanding here;
If this word-shifting has purpose, it's to make you gasp.
Each molds words to make one world,
Sometimes without design makes worlds so becoming
To another that a touch comes true
And gazes at the other, wondering how the words
Were taken from a spirit and given back
With the same rhythm felt in the heart
That takes the measure of your heart's beat.

Muse of my spirit, you, love, the farthest reaches
Of flesh and mind of dreams,
All I could do it seems I did
To say yes to life and a lively movement
To my arrangements of words.
But I remember too the few glimpses
In odd moments of vast ceremonial time
That gut and memory see,
Letting us experience the stormy weather
From that deep existence,
The rite of the season, even the hour of a day,
The moment of the bell's vibrato in its tower
Trembling rose petals in the garden below.

This muse in the mind is a trickster
        for those who follow trends
        and don't we all?
So, for our comfort—say, "Farewell, Muse."

I tried, sometimes I gave up, gave over, but
Overall I tried, and now, though I don't feel old
My years and noisy joints vote yes.
I climbed my prideful mountain,
And stand watch from the escarpment.
The avalanche hovering through my years
Is collapsing now, but isn't that the thought
Of each one caught in the theft in every cycle?

ii.
This awkward grace had shamed me,
That caring my carry us through,
To not pretend, to sing my good tunes here

       for the lies the lies the lies
       where I came to love and how

       cautioned too–my books
       my soap my haircut my acne
       my flag and trumped up words my last resort.

To be here, to speak glyph and tone;
Wind scatters seed, birds may as well speak Latin.
Finding a harmony across distances is the last hope,
As our certainty and our arrogance
Hold hands through night.
All I have all you have
Is the light of this day,
The cadence in this chance.

Here words dance, and the planet sings,
Light sways melody along the tracery of stars.

Hold a few of these words…

    …and me.

Banish that fat smile,
Attend your vision's garden
And embrace the words
Your world is strung upon

Surveying round our bleak horizons.
Yet finding still a certain joy—
The beating wing, a sound of weather

A seed carried through harsh weather
To next year's surprise.

So, there it is.   Beloved.

And here I abandon it to you…

STEPHEN WIEST was born the day after Pearl Harbor. He has worked as a janitor, bartender, Fuller Brush salesman, printer, and gardener for people who like flowers but not dirt. He studied with Elliott Coleman, and in the late sixties was Poet in Residence at The Johns Hopkins University. Early poems were published by Cid Corman in Japan, and the origin of Screeds was published by Denis Boyles in Switzerland in the sixties. This final version of Screeds is his first publication in twenty-six years. He has written five books of poetry and four novels. He spends most of his time playing in his garden in Rock Hall, Maryland, an old waterman's town on the Chesapeake Bay, and watching eagles and hummingbirds on Eastern Neck Island. He has two sons and has been married a long time to Susan, a successful businesswoman, for whom he tries to be socially acceptable.

ABOUT THIS EDITION.

The copies of this edition printed for
subscribers of The Fortnightly Review are numbered.

This is number:

Copies for general distribution are unnumbered.

THE FORTNIGHTLY REVIEW
[New Series.]

ODD VOLUMES

Our imprint is named in memory of The Sette of Odd Volumes, a
celebrated and long-lived association of bibliophiles founded in London
in 1878 by Bernard Quaritch and others. Our colophon and other
devices are borrowed from some of the Sette's early
printed pieces.

http://fortnightlyreview.co.uk
http://oddvolumes.co.uk

Made in the USA
Lexington, KY
12 March 2015